Reflections

N.C. Thomas

Reflections © 2023 N.C. Thomas

All rights reserved.

No part of this publication may be reproduced, stored in a retrieval system, or transmitted, in any form or by any means, electronic, mechanical, photocopying, recording, or otherwise, without the prior written permission of the presenters.

N.C. Thomas asserts the moral right to be identified as the author of this work.

Presentation by *BookLeaf Publishing*

Web: www.bookleafpub.com

E-mail: info@bookleafpub.com

ISBN: 9789357214650

First edition 2023

*To my Mother and Father and to all my
Loved Ones*

I

If longing is wrong
Then I am a sinner
With black heart
And heavy hand

Bestowed a tongue of lead
Too heavy to speak
Eyes of stone
Too stubborn to move

The scene of endless green
A paradise the Israelites
Had never seen
An obscene fantasy

II

An ant works hard all day
But when is there time for play?
Even when you are close,
I feel like you are away.
From a world so foreign to mine,
Is there any chance you stay?

III

3

Sowers sow seeds that
Take years to grow

And a thousand years
Are like yesterday to
He who knows

It is not I who opens
My lips, but a wicked,
Deceitful worm

I await thee at the
Midnight hour, come and
Build me firm

Strong as an oak which
Takes years to grow

IV

In Carmel-
By-the-Sea
You come my way
Elegantly

Grace flutters
By my ears,
All of a sudden
Disappears

With things
To do, a
Mission to fulfill its
Beauty cannot linger,
Still

V

5

Fare thee well, friend?
It has been so long,
One might say he knows
Thee not!

Fare me well has
Been all for naught

How could this be?
The last seen of
Thee was
Thine flourishing family!

Woe is me, for my
Family is no longer in
My company

How is this so?
Disease, famine or a
Visit from Below?

For me? No.
It began in Bordeaux, where
I hath had the disposition to
Outgrow

Thou sayeth that
Thou hath had? Man knoweth
Himself least of all!
Fare thee well, Conrad.

VI

7

Do you hear us?
We cry out your name.
But now, you are so tall
That even Liberty, you cannot hear.

Just like the dead
With finality, all
Hope is lost.
Still, we fall.

Do you know you are blind?
Racing towards emptiness
Alone.
Even if you reach the stars,
You will still freeze and die
Alone.

Do you see what you have done?
Does it come as a surprise
That you have caused all our demise?

Still, we fall.

VII

This land to which mine eyes see fairest,
Created with care by the One above
When will thine bosom become most barest?
Canst thou giveth me ones that I might love?
As very beauteous as thou canst be,
Fulfillment is not found in thine arms
Thou canst not replace faith and family.
For glory and adventure have such charms
These things, they stir the souls of those ruin'd
men
Whose lives they squander on frivolous ends.
Taking man from wife, father from children
How canst one forgive? Who wilt make
amends?
Forgive, for man has a great duty here,
Incline, to Our Father, his ear to hear.

VIII

9

How is one a friend?
Well I don't know. Please tell me.
You cannot pretend.

IX

Under the willow tree
Sit you and me
Waiting for the time
To come.
When all is made right
When there is an
Illumined night
Many have waited
And still more will
Wait
For ever and ever
Unto ages of ages

X

Pride, a cunning and
Cruel master.
King of the sins, as is right.
From it, are bestowed
Gifts, with delight.

A challenge to Pride
Is first among insults.
The man challenged
Is the first among dolts.

Man paints himself in his
Own image, but when the
Paint splatters, he only
Leaves a wreckage.

A soul is a precious thing.
It is hard to keep when one
thinks himself, the Beginning.

When all a man has
Is his Pride, it might
Just be better
if he died.

XI

Man at head of his table
Foundation is unstable

Mother out at stable
She tells fable

Son is disable

XII

Smoke rises day and night
The fragrance fills
The nostrils of those
Who come.

The bell tolls and
the victims mourn.
How could they have
been so dumb?

Only those who
Had the might
Would be able to
Succumb.

But they are not
Alone. Many approach,
Coming from the walls,
Singing an anthem.

The heart which
Is aflame, the
One filled with fight
Will not drum
For that Vile one.

XIII

It is my fault, yes?
It is your fault. Are we done?
I wish we were not.

XIV

15

We march unto our death
And by death we all trample
Down their hope and their breath.
How can this be? An example:
Snowflakes fall to their eternal rest.
One by one they cover the ground.
Life, then, is at their behest.
Just the same, for yours, we are bound.

XV

The Sloth, a benevolent master.
He brings blessings
of peace, he does not stir.
Ignorance, he also brings.
O, master! Show me your
Ways! Enlighten me with
Peace! Please, my savior!
I've heeded the legend, the myth!
How is it that an answer be given
When the master is lord of indolence?
How is it that any could be chosen
When, in reality, he is a dunce?
How can one that is empty
Give anything at all?
A way that is foolish and beastly
Will only lead to another fall.
True blessings, to feel and to love,
Are so rejected by those
That hate and loathe the One above.
He who thinks he knows
Will end his life comfortably
But he will also reject his Humanity.

XVI

A man, standing guard at the city gate,
Does his job and protects his community,
A man that does his duty.
He has always pulled his weight.
One day, at noon, came a young girl.
She went, shyly, slowly, to the guard
and said with a quick twirl,
"I brought this flower from my yard,
It's for all the hard work you do,
Protecting me and my family too."
The guard was shocked!
How sweet a gesture to receive.
He tried to speak, then a bird squawked.
"I've been so naïve!"
Said he. Later that evening, while he ate,
His children asked about the gate.
"We are here together, all!
I cannot defend alone,
for then I am small!
Here we are each other's own."

XVII

The end is coming, it is near.
Closer than you might think.
To those you love, adhere.
Your life you might link with
Career, hobbies, or goals.
What have you accomplished?
It will not matter when the coals
Start to burn. You will be anguished
But they will never touch your lips.

XVIII

18

On the Blue Danube
I had, then, received a kiss
From eternity

www.ingramcontent.com/pod-product-compliance
Lightning Source LLC
LaVergne TN
LVHW050311200726

843509LV00015B/3268